THE WORLD OF ENERGY

Understanding
GEOTHERMAL ENERGY
and BIOENERGY

FIONA REYNOLDSON

Gareth Stevens
Publishing

Please visit our Web site, www.garethstevens.com. For a free color catalog of all our high-quality books, call toll free 1-800-542-2595 or fax 1-877-542-2596.

Library of Congress Cataloging-in-Publication Data

Reynoldson, Fiona.
Geothermal energy and bioenergy / Fiona Reynoldson.
    p. cm. — (The world of energy)
Includes index.
ISBN 978-1-4339-4121-4 (library binding)
1. Geothermal resources—Juvenile literature. 2. Biomass energy—Juvenile literature.
I. Title.
GB1199.5.R49 2011
621.44—dc22

2010015844

This edition first published in 2011 by
Gareth Stevens Publishing
111 East 14th Street, Suite 349
New York, NY 10003

Copyright © 2011 Wayland/Gareth Stevens Publishing

Editorial Director: Kerri O'Donnell
Art Director: Haley Harasymiw

Photo Credits:
AEA Technology, Harwell: 11, 16, 17 top, 17 bottom, 23 top, 25, 27 right, 29. Ecoscene: 12 (Nichol), 4 (Gryniewicz), 7 (Ayres), 9 (Alan Brown), 10 (Sally Morgan), 10-11 (John Corbett) 27 left (Ford), 28 left (Platt), 28 right (Gryniewicz), 31 (Jim Winkley), 36 (Kevin King), 40 (Joel Creed), 41 (Sally Morgan), 42 (Moore). James Davis Travel Photography: 5, 19, 30 left, 30 right. Eye Ubiquitous: 14 (David Cumming), 24 (Dean Bennett) 34 (L. Johnstone). Olë Steen Hansen: 6, 32. Mary Evans Picture Library: 15. Oxford Scientific Films: 18 (Richard Packwood), 43. Shutterstock.com *cover* and 1 (Johann Helgason); US Department of Energy: 20, 23 bottom, 38, 39 left, 39 right.

Printed in China
CPSIA compliance information: Batch #WAS10GS: For further information contact Gareth Stevens, New York, New York at 1-800-542-2595.

CONTENTS

▲ *Twigs burst into flames when they touch the hot rock on the island of Lanzarote. Here, the underground hot rock comes to the surface.*

Geothermal Energy

Geothermal energy is heat deep underground. The center of the Earth is very hot. It is so hot that it melts the rock around it. A lump of this super-hot rock, about the size of a mountain, has enough heat energy in it to power the whole world for a year. If we could turn more of this hot energy into electricity, it would be very useful.

Geothermal Power Around the World

About 25 countries use geothermal power. The largest users are the United States and the Philippines. Other users of geothermal power include New Zealand, Russia, Mexico, Italy, Japan, Indonesia, and Turkey.

But geothermal power only provides 0.3 percent of the world's electricity. Most electricity is produced by burning fossil fuels (coal, oil, and gas) in power plants.

▲ *A geothermal power plant in Iceland. Hot rocks underground heat water and make steam. The steam turns turbines that power generators, to make electricity. Then the steam cools down to make hot water that is put into a lake. The water is hot enough for people to bathe in it.*

FACT FILE

WHAT'S A WATT?

Scientists measure electrical energy in joules. Using one joule per second is called one watt, for instance, a 40-watt light bulb uses 40 joules for every second it is switched on.

A kilowatt =
 one thousand watts.

A megawatt =
 one million watts.

A gigawatt =
 a billion watts.

Bioenergy

Bioenergy is power produced from plants and animals. Enough plants grow every year to meet the world's energy needs eight times over. Also, plants produce seeds so they renew themselves, unless we use them up too fast.

Green plants make their own food. They use:
- sunlight (solar energy)
- water (from the soil)
- carbon dioxide (from the air).

We can burn plants for light, heat, and cooking. We can make clothes and tools from plants. We can even build houses from plants. ▼

Green leaves

Sun

Sunlight

Carbon dioxide

Sugars and starch produced in the leaves

Plant burned

Plant rots

Plant eaten by animals

Water from roots

Plant digested

▲ *Green leaves make sugars and starches (food for the plant) by using sunlight, carbon dioxide, and water.*

How a Plant Makes Its Food

A plant uses solar energy, water, and carbon dioxide to make food. This is called photosynthesis. The plant can then use the food. We can eat plants and so use their energy. We can also burn plants to give us energy as heat. By burning plants in power plants, we can change their energy into electricity. It would be useful if we could make electricity directly from plants.

▲ *Seaweed is a very common plant. In the future, it may be used at power plants to make electricity.*

GEOTHERMAL ENERGY AND BIOENERGY

The Earth is made up of:

- *a solid metal inner core*
- *a liquid metal outer core*
- *a thick mantle that moves like warm toffee*
- *a thin, solid, cool crust of rock.*

Everything is very hot (except the crust with the continents and oceans on top of it). ▼

What Does Geothermal Mean?

The word *geothermal* comes from two Greek words:

geo = earth   *therme* = heat

So it is used to describe heat from the Earth.

Where Does the Heat Come From?

Most of the energy that heats the Earth's core comes from nuclear reactions taking place inside the Earth. Luckily, there is a cool, outer crust for us to live on.

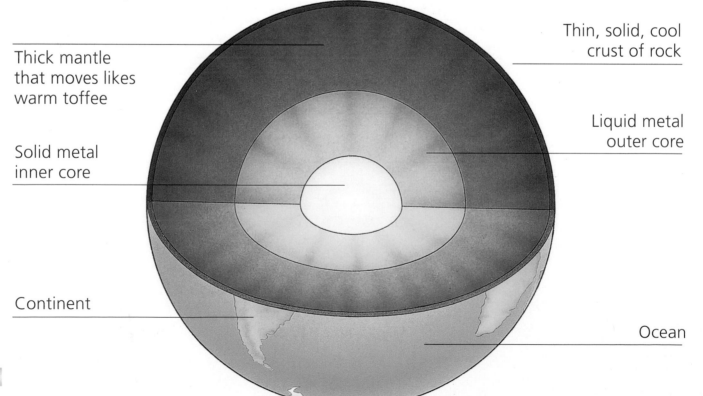

Thin, solid, cool crust of rock

Thick mantle that moves likes warm toffee

Solid metal inner core

Liquid metal outer core

Continent

Ocean

Geothermal Heating

Heat comes up from the core. But it gets cooler and cooler as it nears the surface crust. When it reaches the crust, the heat is let off or radiated into space. We do not notice the geothermal heating, because the heat from the sun is greater.

FACT FILE

The Earth's crust that we live on is like huge pieces of odd-shaped paving stone. Each piece of stone is called a plate. The plates move slowly over the mantle. They carry the continents on top of them.

Tenerife is a Spanish island. It is made of ash and lava from volcanoes. Volcanoes erupt and bring up red-hot material from deep underground.

◄ *This lichen is growing on a tree trunk. Lichens grow all over the world. Local people often burn them as fuel for heating and cooking.*

Where Do Biofuels Come From?

Biofuels come from:

- trees
- shrubs
- grasses
- peat from bogs
- seaweed
- mosses and lichens
- animal dung (often contains bits of plants).

These biofuels are all around us. Huge forests cover parts of North America, Northern Europe, and Asia. Other forests cover large parts of South America, Africa, and the Far East. Apart from forests, there are large areas of grassland and shrubs in the world.

This is a photograph of forest and grassland in a cold part of Sweden. Even in cold places, some plants grow well. They could be used to make fuel. ▼

◀ *These are pine logs. The wood will be used for building. The waste wood chips and bark can be burned as fuel to make electricity.*

The Effects of Geothermal Energy

Geothermal energy drives the very slow movement of the continents (see the Fact File on page 9). The movement of the continents is called continental drift. As the continents drift, they knock into each other, which can cause mountains to be pushed up. If the continents pull apart instead, huge valleys can be formed. All this happens over many millions of years.

Volcanoes show that geothermal energy can also move fast. Volcanoes erupt. They throw up red-hot lava, gas, and ash from the super-hot rock inside the Earth.

FACT FILE

There are about 850 active volcanoes in the world today. Most of them are in the Pacific Ocean.

◄ *This photograph shows rivers of red-hot lava on the islands of Hawaii in the Pacific Ocean. The islands were made from volcanoes that grew up from the ocean floor.*

Snow-Capped Volcanoes

Volcanoes can form high mountains, so they can have snow on the top. If the volcano erupts, the snow mixes with the red-hot lava and ash. It makes a river of mud. This can flow down the mountain and wash whole villages away.

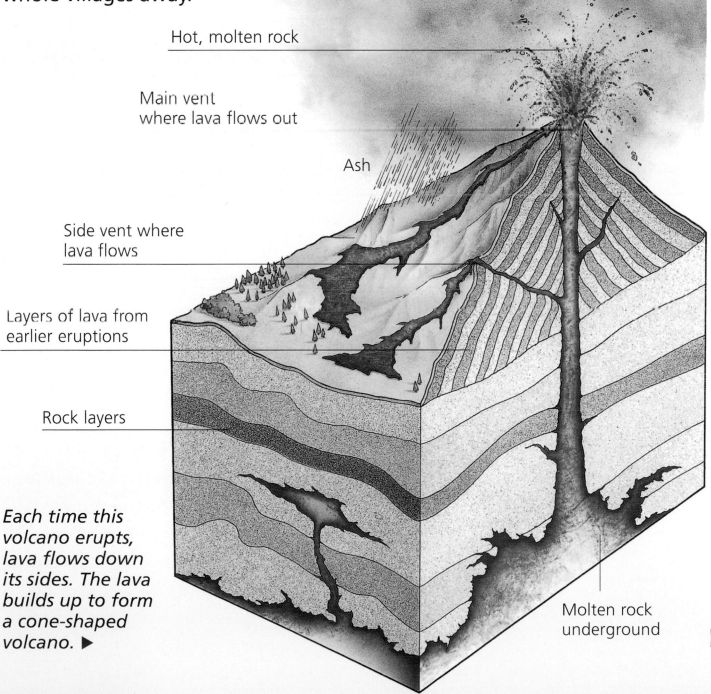

Hot, molten rock

Main vent
where lava flows out

Ash

Side vent where
lava flows

Layers of lava from
earlier eruptions

Rock layers

Molten rock
underground

Each time this volcano erupts, lava flows down its sides. The lava builds up to form a cone-shaped volcano. ▶

13

GEOTHERMAL ENERGY AND BIOENERGY IN HISTORY

Wood-Burning Bioenergy

For thousands of years people have burned wood. This has kept them warm and cooked their food. In many developing countries, wood fires are still the only way of cooking and heating.

A family in northwest India sits around a wood fire. Wood is the most important fuel for millions of people. ▼

Garbage and Gas Bioenergy

In some countries, garbage is burned to make electricity. Also, gas from rotting plants has been used as a fuel.

Geothermal Power

In some places, underground water is heated by geothermal energy. The water comes to the surface as a hot spring (see page 30). The Romans built bathhouses wherever they found hot springs. They enjoyed having hot baths and thought the minerals in the water were good for their health. They built hot spring bathhouses all across the Roman empire.

This is an eighteenth century picture. It shows hot spring baths. Hot springs often have minerals in them, and people thought these were good for them. They sat in the water for hours, or breathed in the steam. ▼

What Is Peat?

Mosses grow well in wetlands (bogs). As they die, they sink. Then they are squashed by new mosses growing on the top. Slowly, the dead mosses build up in layers. They form what is called peat. There are peat bogs all over the world. About one-third of all of Finland is peat bog. Canada, Ireland, and Russia all have a lot of peat.

Peat bogs can be many yards thick. The peat can be cut into bricks. It can be burned on fires or in power plants to make electricity. ▼

◄ *This photograph shows piles of hand-cut blocks of peat. In the past, peat was always dug by hand.*

FACT FILE

Things do not rot much in peat bogs. Animals and humans who fell into bogs thousands of years ago are still well preserved. Hundreds of human bodies dating from over 2,000 years ago have been found in bogs all over Europe.

Peat as a Fuel

Nowadays peat is used in power plants to make electricity for the following places:

- most of Finland's inland cities
- about one-fifth of homes and factories in the Irish Republic
- some parts of Russia
- some parts of the United States.

Peat is now dug out by machines. Apart from fuel, its uses have included bricks for building, and material for mopping up oil spills. ▶

GEOTHERMAL ENERGY AND BIOTECHNOLOGY

Hot Wells

Hot rocks lying underground can be reached by drilling. Then underground water flowing over the rock will be heated. The hot water can be brought up to the surface and used to make electricity.

A muddy pool heated by underground rocks, in Iceland. ▼

The geothermal power plant makes, or generates, electricity from the hot water that comes up the second hole from underground. ▼

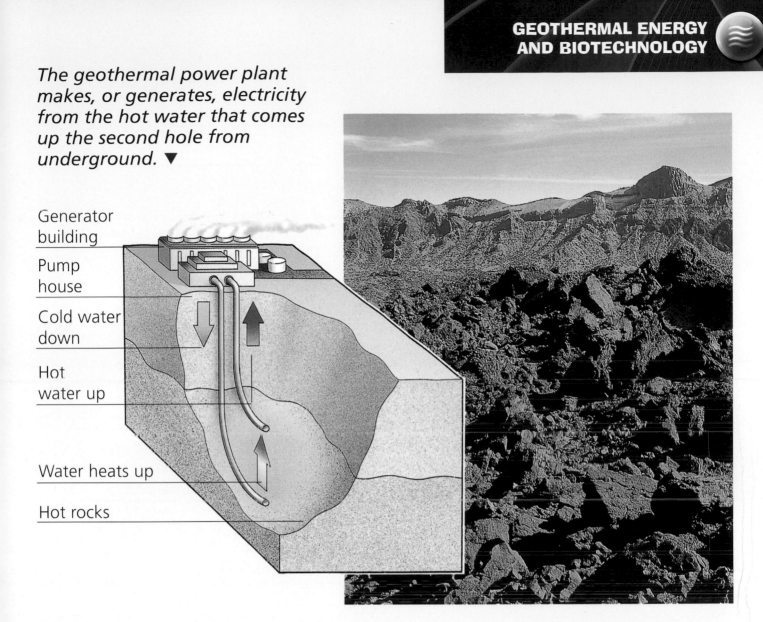

Generator building

Pump house

Cold water down

Hot water up

Water heats up

Hot rocks

Making a Hot Well

The hot rocks underground may be dry, so this is what engineers do.

- They drill two holes.
- Cold water is pumped down the first hole.
- The hot underground rocks heat the water up.
- Then the hot water comes back up the second hole (see the diagram above).

▲ *These lava fields on the island of Tenerife show that there was once a volcano here. The volcano may be so old that the hot rock is far below the surface now.*

Los Alamos National Laboratory

The Los Alamos National Laboratory is in Los Alamos, New Mexico. In 1986, two wells were drilled into the rock there.

Cold water was pumped down a hole into a big, natural space in the rock (see the diagram on page 21). The hot rocks under the ground heated the water. The hot water, or steam, was forced up the second hole. It was about 374 degrees Fahrenheit (190 degrees Celsius) when it came to the surface.

▲ *This photograph shows a geothermal power plant in California.*

In the Power Plant

The power plant was on the surface, above the pipes. In the power plant, the heat was taken out of the water. It was used to make electricity. Then the cooled water was pumped back down the first hole, and heated up again.

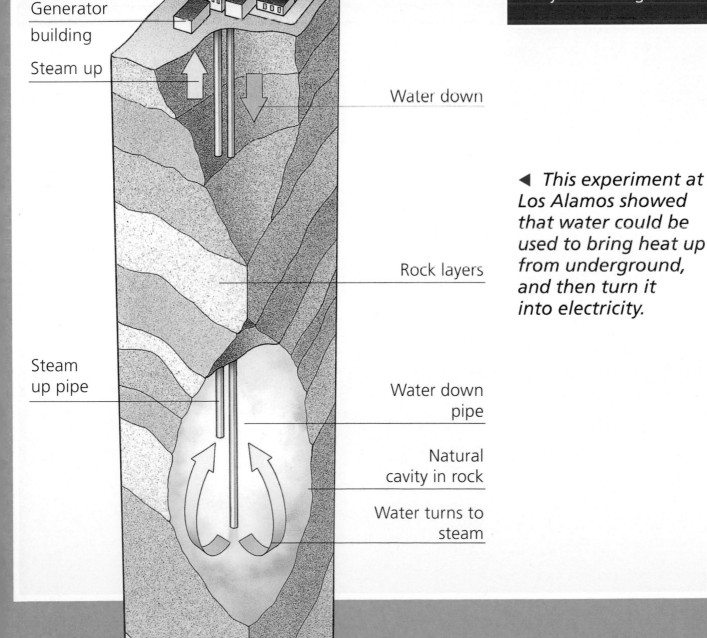

Generator building

Steam up

Water down

Rock layers

Steam up pipe

Water down pipe

Natural cavity in rock

Water turns to steam

◄ *This experiment at Los Alamos showed that water could be used to bring heat up from underground, and then turn it into electricity.*

Burning

In some countries there is plenty of wood, so wood is burned to warm houses and for cooking. Often in sawmills and paper mills, waste bits of wood are burned to heat the building, dry new timber, and to make electricity (see the diagram below). We can burn other garbage in special containers that do not allow the air around it to be polluted.

Burying

There is quite a lot of plant material in everyday household garbage (often about one-third). Household garbage has always been buried on waste ground. But now that there is so much, we are running out of places to bury it.

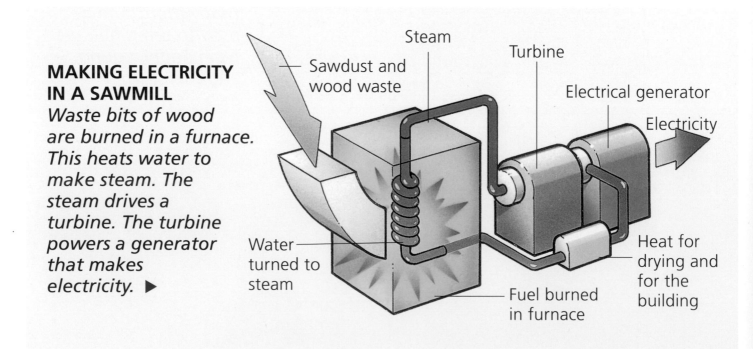

MAKING ELECTRICITY IN A SAWMILL
Waste bits of wood are burned in a furnace. This heats water to make steam. The steam drives a turbine. The turbine powers a generator that makes electricity. ▶

Steam

Turbine

Sawdust and wood waste

Electrical generator

Electricity

Water turned to steam

Fuel burned in furnace

Heat for drying and for the building

▲ Straw from crops such as wheat can be burned to make heat.

◄ This power plant in California burns wood and farm garbage to make electricity.

Animal Dung

Bacteria are tiny bugs. They are so tiny that you cannot see them unless you look through a microscope. Some bacteria grow well in covered tanks. These bacteria are used to rot down animal dung. This makes a gas.

In India and China, people often collect animal dung to use as fuel. They put it into tanks. Bacteria break down the dung and gas is given off. This gas can be used for cooking, heating, and even driving generators to make electricity.

Hundreds of thousands of animals are kept for farming in Africa and Asia. Their dung can be rotted to make gas, or dried to burn as a fuel. ▼

Gas from Waste or Dung

The gas produced from rotting waste or dung is called methane. Some methane gas is collected and used to make electricity in the UK. But methane gas is only a small part of all the UK's electricity supply.

- About 2 percent comes from methane collected at human sewage works.
- About 5 percent comes from methane collected from rotting garbage. Burning garbage also gives about 7 percent.

This photograph shows methane being made at a sewage works. ▶

This diagram shows methane being made by bacteria from slurry (liquid animal dung). ▼

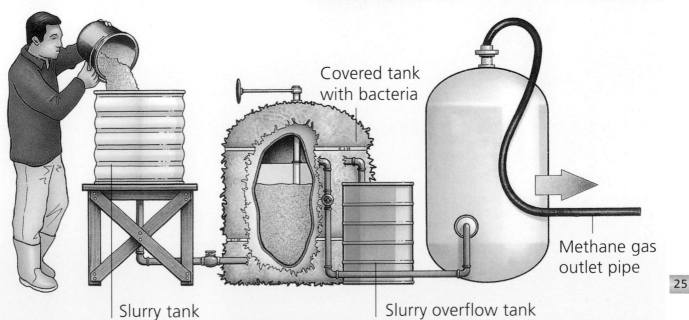

Covered tank with bacteria

Methane gas outlet pipe

Slurry tank

Slurry overflow tank

Problems with Bioenergy

Peat bogs take thousands of years to form.
So digging peat from them destroys the peat bog.

Trees can grow fairly quickly. But in many places, people are cutting trees down and burning them more quickly than new trees can grow. And stripping trees from the land leaves the earth bare. Then wind can blow the earth away. Heavy rain can wash the earth away. This is happening in many parts of the world such as Africa, India, and South America.

As more and more people live on the Earth, they use more and more wood. This map shows the places where there is a shortage of wood. ▼

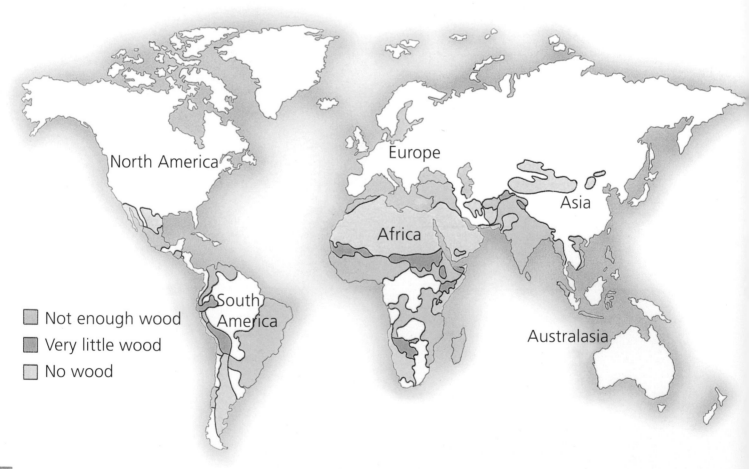

North America

Europe

Asia

Africa

South America

Australasia

☐ Not enough wood
■ Very little wood
☐ No wood

Collecting wood. Burning wood and peat give off carbon dioxide in the same amounts as living trees do. Fossil fuels give off masses of extra carbon dioxide that has been stored in the ground for years as coal, oil, and gas. ▼

Global Warming

Many people think that the Earth's atmosphere is heating up. This is called global warming. It could be happening because we are burning so many fossil fuels, trees, and peat. All these things give off carbon dioxide when they are burned. The big increase in carbon dioxide could be causing global warming.

Household garbage sacks about to be buried. When they have rotted, the gas given off can be used. ▼

◄ *Natural hot water from underground or waste water from a power plant can heat greenhouses.*

A geothermal power plant in Kenya. ▶

Good Things About Geothermal Power

Geothermal power plants are kinder to the environment.

- They use heat from underground that is renewable (will not get used up).
- They produce little or no harmful gases.
- They produce little or no harmful waste materials.

Bad Things About Geothermal Power

Geothermal power does have some problems. Geothermal power plants take water from the ground. This could make the natural level of water in the ground become too low. The ground would dry out and shrink. Then land would start sinking. So water has to be pumped back underground all the time.

Underground gases can escape, too. They can cause air pollution, and be very noisy.

FACT FILE

The geothermal power station on the island of Hawaii produces as much power as 144,000 barrels of oil would produce. The island does not need so much oil brought to it in large oil tankers.

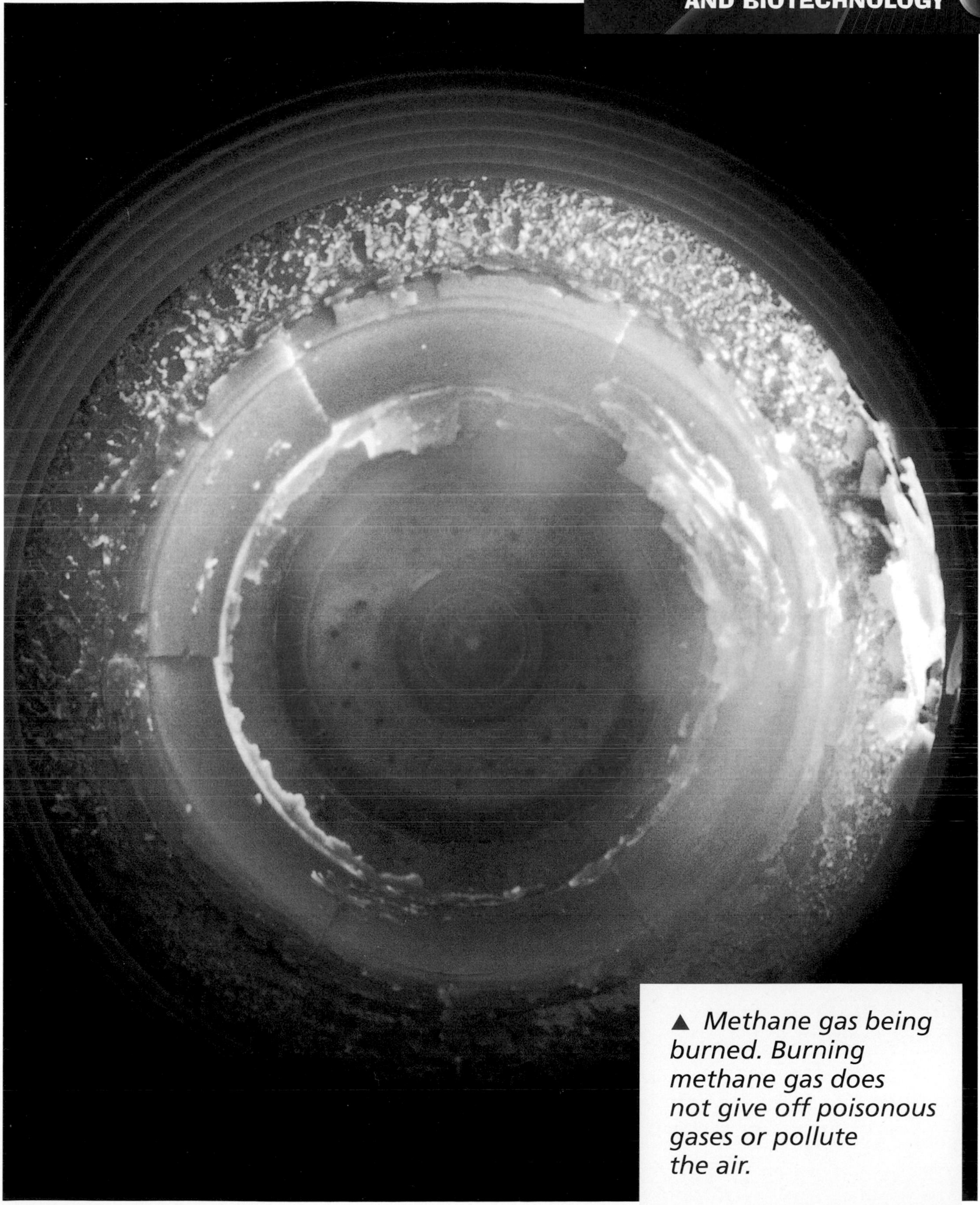

▲ Methane gas being
burned. Burning
methane gas does
not give off poisonous
gases or pollute
the air.

▲ *A bubbling, hot mud pool in Iceland.*

▲ *There are natural hot springs in Bath, UK, from an old volcano. The Romans built bathhouses near the hot spring.*

Hot Springs

Water can be heated by hot underground rocks. When the water comes to the surface it forms hot springs. These are common in volcanic areas such as Iceland and New Zealand.

In some places, fine dust mixes with the hot springs. This forms bubbling, hot mud pools.

The Romans

The Romans discovered hot springs in Baden-Baden, Germany, and built baths there. They not only bathed in the water, they piped the hot water from the springs to heat all their bath buildings.

Iceland

Today, some buildings in the capital city of Iceland are heated by water piped from nearby hot springs.

FACT FILE

In 1883, workers were building the Canadian Pacific Railroad. They saw a huge column of smoke in the distance. When they got closer, they found it was not smoke but steam. It came from boiling-hot underground water. This is called a geyser. Soon people came to see it, and other geysers.

There are many hot springs in the Yellowstone National Park in Wyoming. Here water flows down a hill. Brightly colored algae grow in some of the pools. ▶

TALLEST GEYSERS
The tallest currently:
Steamboat Geyser,
Yellowstone National
Park, U.S.A., 377 feet
(115 meters)
The tallest ever
recorded: Waimangu
Geyser, New Zealand,
1,509 feet (460 meters)

A geyser on the island of Lanzarote.

USING GEOTHERMAL ENERGY AND BIOENERGY

How a Geyser Works

Water trickles down a crack in the ground. It falls onto the red-hot rocks underground. The water boils and flashes to steam. The water and steam are forced up, and meet more cold water coming down. Now all the water and steam is blasted out of the ground in a huge jet.

Where Geysers Are in the World

Most geysers are in New Zealand, Iceland, the United States, and Russia.

The word geyser comes from Geysir in Iceland. Geysir is one of the most spectacular geysers in the world. Every five to 36 hours, there is a jet of steam and water 197 feet (60 m) high.

▲ *Yellowstone National Park in Wyoming has more geysers close together than in any other part of the world.*

Yellowstone National Park

The oldest national park in the world is Yellowstone National Park in Wyoming. The park land is full of old volcanoes. The rocks below the ground are very hot. This means there are many hot springs, boiling mud pools, and geysers. The most famous geyser is Old Faithful, which erupts regularly.

▲ *Thousands of tourists visit Yellowstone National Park every year to watch Old Faithful in action.*

Old Faithful

Some facts about this geyser:

- It erupts every 37–93 minutes.
- It can shoot up to 170 feet (52 m) high.
- It blasts about 10,566 gallons (40,000 L) of water into the air.

Deep underground, water is flowing down cracks toward the red-hot rocks. The heat will flash the water to steam and blast it out of the ground. ▼

Geothermal Power Plants

Countries leading the way with geothermal power plants include the United States, the Philippines, Mexico, Italy, Iceland, and New Zealand. Many other countries worldwide are developing geothermal power, too.

How the Underground Heat Is Used

There are three main ways that underground heat is used.

- Steam from underground directly turns turbines.
- Underground hot water is changed to steam by lowering air pressure and then the steam turns the turbines.
- Underground warm water is used to heat another liquid that boils at a lower temperature and the vapor from this turns the turbines (see the diagram opposite).

Pipes to stop a road freezing in Iceland. Waste hot water from a nearby geothermal power plant can be used to heat everything from greenhouses to road surfaces. ▼

A FLASH PLANT
When the underground water is very hot—347°F (175°C) or more, it is piped to the surface and flashed to steam (by lowering the pressure). Then it turns the turbines. ▶

A BINARY PLANT
When the underground water is hot—212–347°F (100–175°C), it is used to heat another liquid with a lower boiling point than water. Vapor from this liquid drives the turbines. ▼

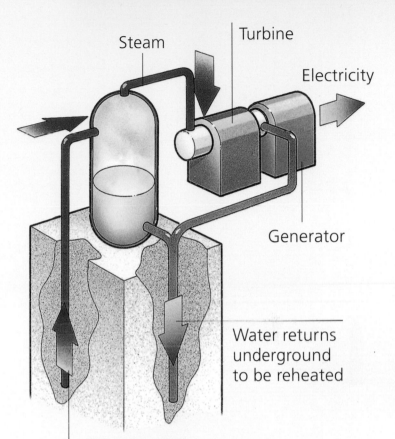

Steam

Turbine

Electricity

Generator

Water returns underground to be reheated

Hot water from underground

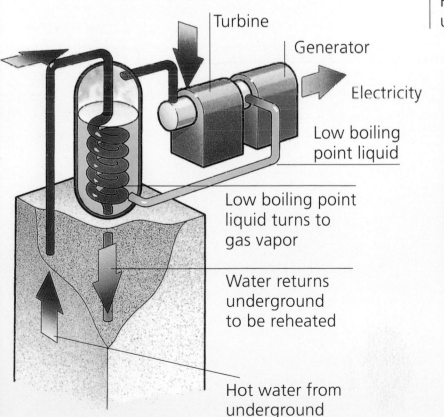

Turbine

Generator

Electricity

Low boiling point liquid

Low boiling point liquid turns to gas vapor

Water returns underground to be reheated

Hot water from underground

FACT FILE

There are 54 geothermal power plants in the U.S.A., making it the world leader in geothermal power. California has 34 plants, Nevada has 16, and Hawaii, Idaho, Utah, and Montana each have one. They provide power for 0.4% of total electricity in the United States.

The Geysers Geothermal Power Plant

The Geysers is built in a volcanic area in California. It first produced electricity in 1960. By 1986, this power plant was supplying more than a million people with their electricity. At full power, it can supply nearly all the electricity needed by San Francisco.

This geothermal power station called The Geysers supplies electricity to people in northern California. ▼

The Geysers' Steam

The rocks under The Geysers are very, very hot. This means that the power plant can use steam straight from the ground.

When the steam has been used, it cools down and becomes water. The water is injected back into the ground to heat up again.

At The Geysers site, steam comes up from underground all the time. ▼

▲ *Drilling is done to find hot rocks underground.*

Plants, Wood, and Rotting Garbage

Both plants and rotting garbage can be used to make liquid or gas fuels. A garbage site begins to produce gas after about three years. It is better if the plant garbage can be separated from other garbage. Plant garbage rots down faster by itself.

Heating wood without much oxygen gives off gases. These gases can be burned inside a gas-turbine engine. The engine's hot gases then heat water in a boiler. This heats water and makes steam. The steam drives the turbines. The turbines drive electricity generators.

▲ *A car in Brazil is filled with gasohol. Gasohol is made from ordinary gasoline and liquids produced from cassava and sugar cane.*

◄ *A fuel alcohol called methanol can be made by heating wood in a tank (gasifier). Chemical changes turn the wood into a liquid.*

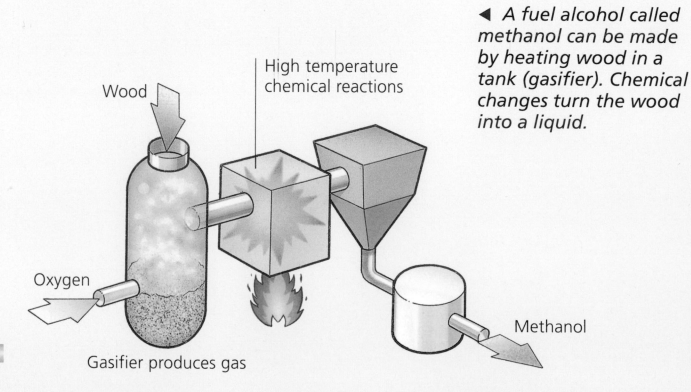

Wood

High temperature chemical reactions

Oxygen

Methanol

Gasifier produces gas

Each sunflower produces a little oil. Thousands of sunflowers can produce enough oil to be a useful fuel. ▼

The Future of Geothermal Power

All countries would like to have energy sources that will not run out. By the end of the twenty-first century, the United States could be getting about one-third of its electricity from geothermal power plants.

Geothermal power stations, such as this one in New Zealand, may become more common in the future. ▼

Geyser Power

It may become possible to use the huge jets from geysers to power turbines directly. It may even be possible to make artificial geysers. This would mean drilling holes in rocks and injecting water into the red-hot rocks below.

▲ *People bathe in hot mud pools on an island near Italy. Many people find this helps to ease muscle pain.*

The Future of Bioenergy

Fuels from plants can be sold to other countries. This would be very useful for poor countries, since geothermal energy can only be used by the country where volcanoes and hot rocks are found. However, local people may be at risk when farm land used for food is taken over to grow fuel crops.

Different Kinds of Plants for Fuel

Many different kinds of plants are being used or developed to make into fuel.

- In Kenya, sugar is being grown for fuel. There are also plans to use Jatropha curcas, a type of shrub.
- At plants in the United States, a fuel called biodiesel is being made from soybean oil. It is also made from other oils such as canola and corn oil.
- Japan is planning to use a biofuel made from the weed camelina to fly aircraft.

Future Filling Stations

In the future, more vehicles will run on different types of fuel. Filling stations will sell more biofuels made from plants and animal waste, such as biodiesel and ethanol.

This picture shows a site using renewable energy sources such as wind power, solar panels, and biogas digesters. In the next hundred years, more of our energy needs will be met in this way. ▶

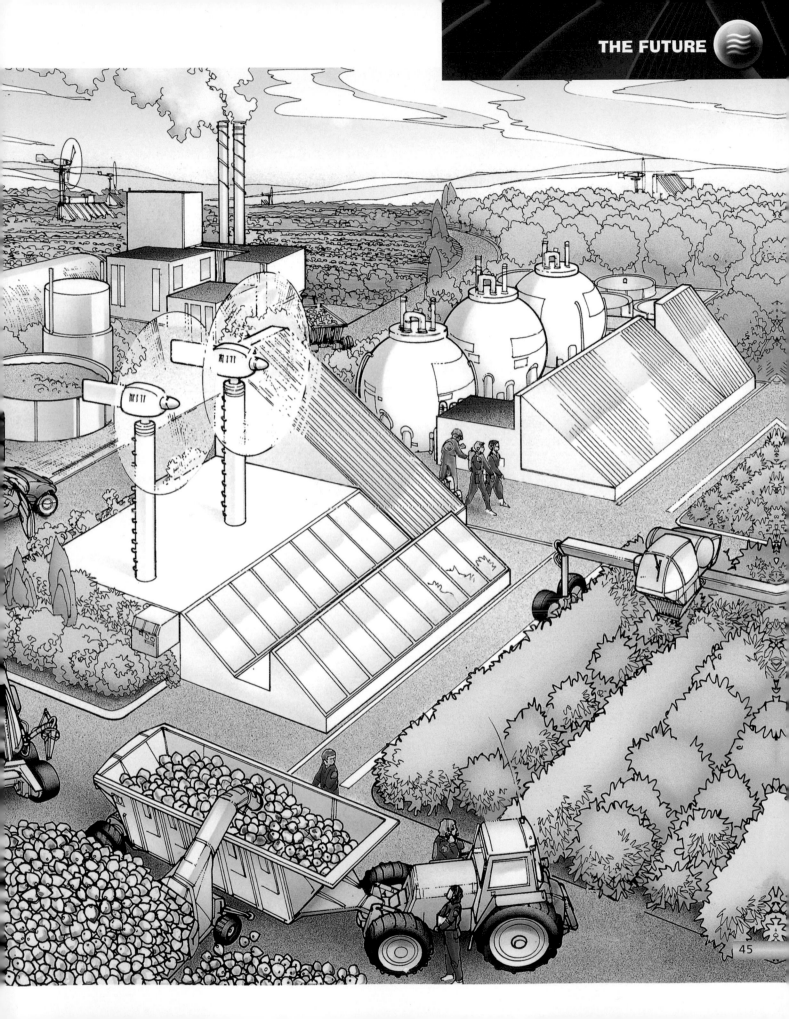

GLOSSARY

Air pollution Dirty air.

Alcohol A liquid that burns easily.

Bacteria Tiny creatures that cannot be seen by the naked eye.

Biodiesel A transportation fuel made from vegetable oils and greases.

Bioenergy Power produced from plants and animals.

Biogas Gas from animal or plant sources.

Carbon dioxide A gas that is present in the air.

Energy The ability to do work.

Ethanol An alcohol fuel made from grains such as corn.

Fossil fuel Coal, oil, or natural gas formed over millions of years from the remains of plants and animals.

Fuel A material that is burned to release the energy that is stored in it.

Gasohol A mixture of alcohol and gasoline.

Generator A machine to produce electricity.

Geothermal Heat from Earth.

Global warming The warming of Earth's atmosphere.

Joule A unit of energy.

Kilowatt One thousand watts.

Megawatt One million watts.

Methane A gas that burns easily. It can be made from rotting material.

Methanol A type of alcohol.

Molten Melted, as in molten rock—so hot that it is liquid.

Natural gas Gas usually found deep underground along with oil deposits.

Power plant A building where energy from a fuel is used to make electricity.

Turbine Blades like a giant fan turned by gas or liquid.

Vapor When a liquid is heated to boiling point it turns to gas. This is called vapor.

Watt A measurement of energy. One watt equals 1 joule being used in 1 second.

Watt-hour One watt being used for one hour. A 40-watt lightbulb used for one hour uses 40 watt-hours of energy.

Further Reading

Energy Today: Geothermal Energy
by Alan Watchel
Chelsea House Publications, 2010

Geothermal Energy: Using Earth's Furnace
by Carrie Gleason
Crabtree Publishing Company, 2008

Powering the Future: New Energy Technologies
by Eva Thaddeus
University of New Mexico Press, 2010

Web Sites

http://home.clara.net/darvill/altenerg/geothermal.htm

http://science.howstuffworks.com/geothermal-energy.htm

http://www.geothermal.org/what.html

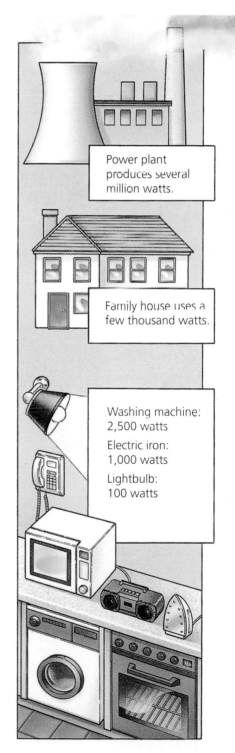

Power plant produces several million watts.

Family house uses a few thousand watts.

Washing machine: 2,500 watts

Electric iron: 1,000 watts

Lightbulb: 100 watts

ENERGY CONSUMPTION
The use of energy is measured in joules per second, or watts. Different machines use up different amounts of energy. The diagram on the right gives a few examples. ▶

INDEX